ABOUT THE BOOK

During an action-packed day David finds many lost objects, aided by silly coincidences that earn him a sudden reputation in the neighborhood of being a boy who can find anything. Returning home to tell his mother of his triumphs, however, produces a surprise ending that will make every reader laugh out loud.

Syd Hoff's sprightly pictures round out Joan Lowery Nixon's droll story.

Joan Lowery Nixon, a noted member of the Mystery Writers of America and the author of many popular books for young readers, has been a free-lance writer and teacher of creative writing for twenty-five years. **Syd Hoff** is the author and illustrator of countless books for children, as well as a cartoonist with an international reputation.

The Boy Who Could Find Anything

a Let Me Read book

Harcourt Brace Jovanovich
New York and London

Weekly Reader Children's Book Club presents

The Boy Who Could Find Anything

By Joan Lowery Nixon

Pictures by Syd Hoff

FOR DOROTHY VAN WOERKOM

Library of Congress Cataloging in Publication Data

Nixon, Joan Lowery.
The boy who could find anything.

(A Let me read book)
SUMMARY: David finds all sorts of missing items for
other people but cannot locate his own possessions.
I. Hoff, Sydney, 1912–   II. Title.
PZ7.N65Bo   [E]   77–15061
ISBN 0–15–210697–9
ISBN 0–15–613748–8 pbk.

David swung back and forth
on the lowest branch
of Mr. Franklin's tree.

Mr. Franklin rubbed his bald head.
"I wonder where my straw hat went,"
he said.

David swung high, and the branch broke.
Down fell David and the branch.

Something fell in his lap.

"Is this your hat, Mr. Franklin?"
David asked.

"Yes!" Mr. Franklin said.
"It must have gotten caught in the tree.
What a smart boy you are
for finding things, David!"

Linda came by on her bike.
"Did you say David is smart
about finding things?"
she asked Mr. Franklin.
"Yes, he is!" Mr. Franklin said.
"He found my hat!"

"Come home with me,"
Linda said to David.
"Help me find my cat."

David walked to Linda's house,
next door to Mr. Franklin's house.

He tripped over the small fence
by the front porch
and fell on his face.

From where he lay on the grass,
he could see under the porch.

"Linda," he said, picking himself up,
"if you look under your porch,
you'll find your cat.
And you'll find something extra.
Your cat had kittens."

Linda got down on the ground.

She looked under the porch.

Then she jumped up.

"Mr. Franklin was right!" she said.
"You are so smart,
you can find anything!"

Mrs. Sanchez leaned out
of her kitchen window.

"Did you say David could find anything?"
she called.

"Could he find my can of pepper?"

David walked across Linda's lawn
to Mrs. Sanchez's house
and into her kitchen.

Mrs. Sanchez was looking
in one of the cupboards.
"I don't know what happened
to my big can of pepper!"
she said to David.
"Please help me find it!"

David saw a bowl of pudding
on the table.
It was warm and spicy
with cinnamon smells.

He put a finger into the pudding
and tasted it
while Mrs. Sanchez wasn't looking.

David made a face.
He stuck out his tongue
and tried to cool it.

Finally he took a deep breath and said,
"Mrs. Sanchez, I think I know
where your can of pepper is.

"I think that your can of pepper
fell into the pudding bowl
when you weren't looking."

Mrs. Sanchez took a spoon
with a long handle
and pulled out the can of pepper.

"Linda was right, David!" she said.
"You are so smart,
you can find anything!"

She dialed the telephone.

"Mr. Adams!" she yelled into the phone.

"I am sending David over to your house.

He can find anything!

He'll help you find your false teeth!"

David walked across the lawn
to Mr. Adams's house next door.

Old Mr. Adams had a hard time
telling David that he couldn't
find his false teeth.

David sat in a chair to think
about where the teeth might be.

He jumped up shouting, "Ouch!"

Mr. Adams's false teeth
were in the chair.

"David!" Mr. Adams said,
as soon as he put in his teeth.
"Mrs. Sanchez was right!
You're so smart,
you can find anything!"

"Who can find anything?"
Tommy asked from the doorway.

"I can," David said.

"Then will you come with me
to my house?" Tommy asked.
"My mother told me
to take care of my little brother.
Only he's hiding from me,
and I can't find him anywhere."

As soon as they were in Tommy's
house next door, David said,
"Where have you looked
for your little brother?"

"Everywhere!" Tommy said.

"Inside and outside!"

"I'll sit here and think very hard
about where he could be," David said.

He flopped on the sofa.

It bent and creaked.

David heard a strange sound
under the sofa.

He stood up and said to Tommy,
"If you look under the sofa,
that's where you'll find him hiding."

Tommy crawled under the sofa
and pulled out his little brother.

"Mr. Adams was right, David!" he said.
"You're so smart,
you can find anything!"

The door flew open,
and Tommy's father, Mr. Greenly,
rushed into the room
waving his briefcase.

"Did I hear you say David is so smart
that he can find anything?" he asked.
"Maybe he can find my speech!
It's not in my briefcase!"

He waved his briefcase so wildly
that David stepped back
into the bookcase.

The bookcase wobbled and shook,
and a book fell off the top.

David tried to catch it, but instead
he caught a handful of papers.

"My speech!" Mr. Greenly said.

"I left it in the dictionary.

David! Tommy was right.

You're so smart, you can find anything!"

David walked out on the front porch.
He watched Mr. Greenly run to his car,
still waving his briefcase.

David hurried home
and into the living room.
"Mom!" he shouted.
"I've got something to tell you!"

"Before you do," his mother said,
"I want you to pick up your shoes."

"What shoes?" David asked.

"The ones right in front of your nose,"
his mother said.

"The ones you thought you had lost."

She held out a paper.

"Here is the homework
you couldn't find this morning.
It was on the table.

"And here is the football
you were looking for—
just where you left it
on the dining room chair.

"Now," his mother asked,

"what was it you wanted to tell me?"

David said happily,
"I just wanted to tell you
that everyone on our block
says I'm so smart,
I can find anything!"

David's mother laughed and laughed.
David wondered why.